T0022806

The *Best* GRANDMOTHER NAMES *Ever*

CHOOSE YOUR PERFECT
GRANDMA NAME,
from Bubble and Gigi
to Memaw and Nana

CATHY LIVINGSTONE

sourcebooks

Copyright © 2009, 2024 by Cathy Caputo Livingstone
Cover and internal design © 2024 by Sourcebooks
Cover and interior art by Caribay M. Benavides

Sourcebooks and the colophon are registered trademarks of Sourcebooks.

All rights reserved. No part of this book may be reproduced in any form or by any electronic or mechanical means including information storage and retrieval systems—except in the case of brief quotations embodied in critical articles or reviews—without permission in writing from its publisher, Sourcebooks.

Published by Sourcebooks
P.O. Box 4410, Naperville, Illinois 60567-4410
(630) 961-3900
sourcebooks.com

Originally published as *Bubbe, Mimi, & Gigi: The Best Grandmother Name Book Ever* in 2009 in the United States of America.

Cataloging-in-Publication Data is on file with the Library of Congress.

Printed and bound in the United States of America.
VP 10 9 8 7 6 5 4 3 2 1

Contents

Foreword

Bubbe, my Irish-Catholic mother, unknowingly initiated the idea for this book. When our daughter was born, my mother announced that she would not be called "Grandma" by her grandchildren, but "Bubbe." My siblings and I thought it was quite comical, since Bubbe is a traditional Jewish grandmother name and we are Catholic. However, the name actually seemed fitting, even though we didn't know the true definition of the name "Bubbe." Notwithstanding any criticism or input from us, my mother prevailed and "Bubbe Caputo" was born.

Introduction

No two grandmothers are alike. Today's grandmothers are women-on-the-go and are playing a significant role in their grandchildren's lives every day. It is important that your "Grandmother" name defines the unique, wonderful grandmother that you are. So why has there never been a helpful book to assist you in choosing the best Grandma name for you?

The grandmother name descriptions that follow each grandma name were derived from many sources: various grandmother stories people shared with me, online grandparent blogs, and my imagination and interpretation of existing grandmothers. The descriptions are intended to be fun, out-of-the-box, and sometimes a little bit silly—and every grandmother name is subject to your creativity, perception, and real-life experiences.

Whether you are already a grandmother or are a grandmother-to-be, many congratulations to you! May this book bring you some laughs and fun moments with your family and friends. Best wishes for a joyous and adventurous Grandmotherhood!

> "When a child is born, so are grandmothers."
>
> —Judith Levy, author

Grandma Name Quiz

Congratulations on your upcoming "Grandmotherhood" journey! Your first exciting step is choosing your special new Grandma name. Your Grandma name is important because you are unique and special—there's only one you! This Quiz will start you on your way to finding the perfect name for you.

Do you drive a:

- **A.** Convertible or sports car
- **B.** SUV or station wagon
- **C.** Hybrid
- **D.** Cadillac, Buick, or 4-door sedan

In your leisure time, you usually:

- **A.** Run marathons, do yoga, or rock climb
- **B.** Shop for clothes
- **C.** Volunteer at a local hospital
- **D.** Knit, sew, or read a book

Your best friend would say your best quality is:

A. Sense of humor

B. Sense of style

C. Sense of smell

D. Sense of direction

What is your favorite vacation?

A. Downhill skiing in the Rockies

B. Sunning yourself at the beach

C. Camping in the middle of nowhere

D. Wine tasting in Europe

Your everyday dress style is mostly:

A. Jeans or sporty clothes

B. Dressy or professional

C. Vintage or "gently worn"

D. Comfy sweats or clothes with elastic waists

You last saw a movie in the movie theater:

A. Last week

B. Last year

C. Not this decade

D. With your first boyfriend

Your favorite shoes are:

A. Sneakers

B. High heels hot off the runway

C. Flip-flops

D. Easy Spirit shoes

At an amusement park, you would:

A. Skip the rides and go directly to the karaoke

B. Ride the Ferris wheel—because you like to be up high

C. Shoot the ducks for a prize

D. Enjoy the carousel ride only

Who would play you in the movie of your life?

A. Jennifer Garner

B. Martha Stewart

C. Whoopi Goldberg

D. Meryl Streep

Your favorite kind of house pet is:

A. Dog or cat

B. Parakeet

C. Chia Pet

D. Goldfish

For Halloween, you like to dress up as a:

A. Witch

B. Playboy Bunny

C. Garage mechanic

D. 1920s flapper

If you were in a music competition, what song would you sing?

A. "Over the Rainbow"

B. "Born in the USA"

C. "YMCA"

D. "I Can't Get No Satisfaction"

Answers

Mostly A

You are very social, outgoing, and are a born leader. Possible Grandmother names for you are: Mimi, Gigi, Dede, Bibi, or Glamma.

Mostly B

You are active, adventurous, and enjoy the outdoors. Possible Grandmother names for you are: Birdie, Coco, Bubbe, Galini, or Vovo.

Mostly C

You are a comedian who loves telling stories and cheering people up. Possible Grandmother names for you are: Manita, Snookie, DaMa, Sassy, or Toot.

Mostly D

You are serious, trustworthy, and a peacemaker amongst friends and family. Possible Grandmother names for you are: Nana, Gram, Lilly, Nonna, or Vela.

Grandmother Names

Aanak	**(pronounced ä-näk).** She can be cold as ice. **Persona:** Husky Grandma
Abba	**(pronounced ä-bbä).** She's a dancing queen. **Persona:** Take-a-Chance-on-Grandma Abba
Abuela	**(pronounced ä-bā-lä).** Literally translated from Spanish, "an old woman grandmother." After a meal at Abuela's house, you are guaranteed to gain a pound or two! **Persona:** Always-Cooking Spanish Grandma **Fun Fact:** Spanish Saying: "No tiene Abuela?" Literally translated as "Have you no Grandmother?" Loosely translated as "Have you no conscience, no shame?"

Abuelita

(pronounced ä-bā-lē-tä). Little gold earrings adorn this grandma. She has a lot to say and speaks quickly, so pay close attention.

Persona: Fast-Talking Grandma

Fun Fact: Sara García, movie star of the 1940s and 50s, is affectionately known as Mexico's Abuelita. Garcia's image appears on the label of Mexico's traditional Abuelita chocolate, which is now owned by Nestle.

Abbey

(pronounced â-bē). In her house, she subscribes to the "Church of Abbey."

Persona: Holier-than-Thou Grandma

Aggie

(pronounced ä-gē). College football fanatic.

Persona: Texas Grandma

Fun Fact: When the Texas A&M yearbook changed its name from The Longhorn to Aggieland, Aggie became the official student body nickname.

"You are never too old to become younger."

—*Mae West, actress*

Airy	**(pronounced â-rē).** Literally translated from English, "graceful, fairylike, and mannered." Airy has an easy, breezy personality. **Persona:** Easy-Going Grandma
Ajax	**(pronounced ā-jăks).** She has always been a workhorse. **Persona:** Good-Work-Ethic Grandma
Aja	**(pronounced ä-jä).** Colorful, flowing fabrics drape Aja. Children marvel at her nose ring. **Persona:** Coast-of-India Grandma
Ama	**(pronounced ä-mä).** She says, "You can Ask Me Anything." **Persona:** Endless-Knowledge Grandma **Fun Fact:** AMA is a social media acronym for Ask Me Anything.
Ame	**(pronounced ā-mä).** A friendly, warm grandmother. **Persona:** Friendly Grandma
AnaGram	**(pronounced ăn-ä-grăm).** An expert crossword & sudoku player. **Persona:** Former English Teacher Grandma

Annanee	**(pronounced änä-nā).** No shoes allowed indoors. **Persona:** Wall-to-Wall-Carpet Grandma
Antsy	**(pronounced ănt-sē).** She's unable to keep still—very impatient with young children. **Persona:** Always-on-the-Move Grandma
Apple	**(pronounced ăp-əl).** "You are the apple of my eye" and "As American as apple pie." **Persona:** Sweet-N-Tart Grandma
Auntie	**(pronounced än-tē).** Auntie suggests she is way too young to possibly be a grandmother. **Persona:** In-Denial Grandma
Austen	**(pronounced ä-stən).** She is majestic and venerable. **Persona:** Romantic Grandma **Fun Fact:** Jane Austen (1775–1817) was an English novelist. Her works of romantic fiction are well-known. She is known today as the "Grandma of Chick Lit."

Actress Julie Andrews is *Grand Julie.*

Avó

(pronounced ä-vō). She has no problem telling you to "stuff-it!"

Persona: Portugal Cork-It Grandma

Fun Fact: Portugal is the world's leading producer of natural cork.

Baachan

(pronounced bă-chän). Literal Japanese translation, "Old Lady."

Persona: Graceful Grandma

Baba

(pronounced bă-bă). Resembling a former heavyweight champion, Baba is a strong woman who tackles problems head-on.

Persona: Headstrong Grandma

Fun Fact: Grandmother Witch "Baba Yaga" is a mythical creature in Russian folklore stories who appears both as a warning to kids to be good and as a source of wisdom.

Babaanne	**(pronounced bä ban ne).** Baklava is her favorite dessert. **Persona:** Sweet-Treat-Baking Grandma **Fun Fact:** Baklava is a traditional pastry dessert that is known for its sweet, rich flavor and flaky texture.
Babci	**(pronounced bop chi).** Her pierogis are a family gathering delicacy. **Persona:** Dumpling-Making Grandma
Babcia	**(pronounced băb-sē-ä).** An outdoorsy woman with a garden everyone envies, she has the gift of making things grow. **Persona:** Green-Thumb Polish Grandma
Babe	**(pronounced bāb).** Because her husband has always affectionately called her "Babe" and so "Babe" it is. **Persona:** Happy Wife

The #1 child care provider today is grandparents.

Babi

(pronounced bä bē). Believes in mystical powers.

Persona: Atheist Grandma

Fun Fact: Czechoslovakia has the highest beer consumption in world.

Babka

(pronounced bäb-kä). Babka cooks from recipes handed down from generation to generation. She will never divulge that secret ingredient!

Persona: Tight-Lipped Grandma

Fun Fact: Babka, a Polish sweet bread, supposedly got its name because its shape is similar to a grandmother—smaller at the top and wider at the bottom.

Babucia

(pronounced bä -boo- shä). Wears her wedding ring on her right ring finger.

Persona: Tunnel-of-Love Ukrainian Grandma

Fun Fact: The Tunnel of Love is located in Klevan, Ukraine. It is a railway surrounded by green arches and is three to five kilometers in length.

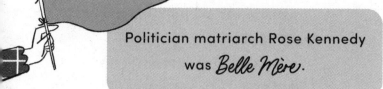

Politician matriarch Rose Kennedy was *Belle Mère*.

Baka	**(pronounced bä kä).** Uses Vegeta to flavor dishes. **Persona:** Bosnian Grandma **Fun Fact:** Vegeta is a basic dry seasoning mix of dehydrated carrots, turmeric, garlic, and salt.
Bamma	**(pronounced bam-ma).** College football fanatic. **Persona:** Alabama Grandma
Bana	**(pronounced bă-nă).** Conservative and plain-looking, she has been recycling for years. **Persona:** Environmentally-Friendly Grandma
BeBop	**(pronounced bē-bop).** 1. A jazz style that was developed in the 1940s. 2. BeBop is never without her sneakers. 3. Athletic and spry, she easily keeps up with her grandkids. **Persona:** In-Shape Grandma

Bebe	**(pronounced bə-bə).** Literal English translation "Baby." **Persona:** Sexy-Young-Looking Grandma **Fun Fact:** Tony Award winner Bebe Neuwirth gained popularity with her portrayal of Dr. Lilith Crane on the hit comedy series *Cheers*.
BeeBee	**(pronounced bē-bē).** BeeBee likes big, straw hats and is someone who rarely complains. **Persona:** No-Worries Grandma
Beanie	**(pronounced bē-nē).** 1. A small, petite hat. 2. A southern belle who is a gracious social butterfly. **Persona:** Southern Social-Climber Grandma
Beeta	**(pronounced bē-tä).** She is not one to scream and to shy away from bugs and insects. Nature is her passion. **Persona:** Outdoors Grandma

Bella

(pronounced běl-lä). Just like her name, Bella is a beautiful grandmother. Just a bit of rouge and a hint of lipstick is all she needs.

Persona: Rosy-Cheeks Grandma

Fun Fact: The name, Bella Donna, is translated as "Beautiful Lady." However, the plant with the same name is known as "Deadly Nightshade."

Belle Mére

(pronounced běl-mər). Literally translated from French, "Mother-in-Law." Belle Mére exudes charm, sophistication, and intelligence.

Persona: Charming French Grandma

Beta

(pronounced bě-tä). Literally translated from English, "a measure of volatility." Beta is always willing to jump in and "test the waters."

Persona: Do-as-I-Say-Not-as-I-Do Grandma

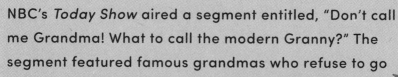

NBC's *Today Show* aired a segment entitled, "Don't call me Grandma! What to call the modern Granny?" The segment featured famous grandmas who refuse to go by the moniker "Grandma."

Bibi	**(pronounced bĭb-bē).** Bibi is a cute grandmother with a big personality. Bibi enjoys outings in the city with her grandkids. **Persona:** Bright-Lights-Big-City Grandma **Fun Fact:** Actress Bibi Besch's famous role was as Dr. Carol Marcus, mother of Captain Kirk's son in *Star Trek II*.
Big Gram	**(pronounced bĭg grăm).** Old-fashioned and down-to-earth. Comfort food, particularly meatloaf and mashed potatoes, is her specialty. **Persona:** Homemaker Grandma
Big Mama	**(pronounced bĭg mä-mä).** A solid, larger-than-life matriarch who can be quite outspoken and somewhat overbearing. **Persona:** Speak-When-Spoken-To Urban Grandma
Big Meme	**(pronounced bĭg memā).** Her life imitates art. **Persona:** Artistic Grandma

Bink

(pronounced bingk). Bink installed an outdoor pool, so her grandchildren would insist on going over to Grandma Bink's house. She's always trying to "one up on" whomever she is with.

Persona: Spare-the-Rod, Spoil-the-Grandchild Grandma

Binky

(pronounced bingk-ē). An eternal optimist. "Every day is a new day" is her motto.

Persona: Glass-Is-Half-Full Grandma

Birdie

(pronounced bŭr-dē). 1. Golf term or small bird. 2. Birdie is someone sporty and "on her game." 3. Preppy pink and lime green clothes are her wardrobe signature.

Persona: The Golf & Tennis Club Grandma

Bitsy

(pronounced bĭt-sē). Doting, loving, and somewhat scatterbrained, she could forget to pick up her grandkids from school due to a tennis match.

Persona: Prep-School Grandma

Bitty	**(pronounced bĭt-dē).** 1. Tiny, petite. 2. Bitty has had secret credit cards in her name for years. **Persona:** Upper-Somewhere Grandma
Bomma	**(pronounced bŏm-mä).** Bomma likes to wear "festive" holiday sweaters. **Persona:** Stay-Out-of-Her-Way Grandma **Fun Fact:** Bomma was a WWII Norwegian freighter vessel.
Bonnie Mamy	**(pronounced bŏn-ē-mā-mī).** Loosely translated from French as "Good Mother." Bonnie Mamy likes to say, "We have quite enough to do weeding our own garden." **Persona:** Old-Belgian-Saying Grandma

"If I'd known how wonderful it would be to have grandchildren, I'd have had them first."

—*Lois Wyse, author*

Bonnie My	**(pronounced bŏn-ē-mī).** Literal Scottish translation, "My Beautiful." Bonnie My is fiercely loyal to her "clan." **Persona:** Beautiful Scottish Grandma **Fun Fact:** "My Bonnie Lies over the Ocean" is a traditional Scottish folk song.
Boo	**(pronounced bōō).** Able to easily startle anyone. **Persona:** Suddenly-There Grandma
Bootsy	**(pronounced bōōt-sē).** To boot = to kick. Behave or else she'll "bootsy" you! **Persona:** Kick-Ass Grandma
Booty	**(pronounced bōōt-tē).** 1. A valuable prize or award. 2. Sharp and dependable. 3. She never misses her weekly poker game with her friends. **Persona:** Goodfellas Grandma
Bossie	**(pronounced bôs-ē).** Bossie = Bossy. **Persona:** Matriarch Grandma
Bree	**(pronounced brē).** Bree can usually be found with an apron around her waist, a measuring cup in one hand, and a trowel in the other. **Persona:** Martha-Stewart-Wanna-Be Grandma

Bubbe

(pronounced bŭh-bē). She is a great source of Yiddish sayings and has a vivacious personality coupled with down-to-earth values. She can be unpredictable at times, but reliable when it comes to her grandkids.

Persona: Jewish Grandma

Fun Fact: Avrom Honig's 83-year-old grandmother, Bubbe, was the star of her popular online kosher cooking show Feed Me Bubbe.

Celebrity Grandma Story

When Martha Stewart became a grandma, her daughter announced, "My mother is going to be called *Martha*!'... I don't like the term 'Grandma.'"

Bubbles

(pronounced bŭb-əls). 1. Something lacking substance. 2. A bundle of energy with money to spend on her latest boyfriend and, of course, on her grandkids.

Persona: Popular Grandma

Bubu Yalewa	**(pronounced bōō-bōō yölälä).** Plans on carrying on the hot-stone walking tradition. **Persona:** Calloused-Feet-Fijian Grandma
Bunica	**(pronounced bōō nēkä).** Loves castle touring in eastern Europe. **Persona:** Romanian Grandma
Bunko	**(pronounced bun kō).** Bunko with the girls is a weekly nonnegotiable event. **Persona:** Gambling Grandma
Bunny	**(pronounced bə nē).** Super pretty waitress at the local diner. **Persona:** Loves-Serving-Others Grandma
Bunya	**(pronounced bŭn-yä).** Do not be late when visiting Bunya, or you will be in big trouble. **Persona:** Strict Ukrainian Grandma
Buscia	**(pronounced boo shä).** Idolizes Polish Nobel Prize winner Marie Curie. **Persona:** Radioactive Polish Grandma

Buster

(pronounced bŭst-ər). A rather big, husky woman who is not particularly fond of sitting and visiting.
Persona: Crabby Grandma

One Irish-Catholic grandmother with an Italian last name from Boston was determined to be called Bubbe—a traditionally Jewish name for grandmother. Her family thought her idea was comical, but she prevailed and "*Bubbe Caputo*" was born.

C

Caddy

(pronounced kadē). Is able and willing to run errands expediently.
Persona: No-Job-Too-Small-for Caddy

Cadillac

(pronounced kä-dĭ-lək). 1. The best, magnificent. 2. Advice to sons-in-law: Do not mess up and call her "Old Battle-Ax!"
Persona: Maintenance-Free Grandma

CanCan	**(pronounced kăn-kăn).** 1. Lively and risqué dance known for its high kicks. 2. Anything goes at this grandma's house. **Persona:** Permissive Grandma
ChaChi	**(pronounced chă-chē).** She is hard to keep up with! Whether power walking with her friends or taking a yoga class, she is a woman on the go. **Persona:** Former-Phys-Ed-Teacher Grandma
CandyGram	**(pronounced kăndee grăm).** She can persuade you into doing most anything. **Persona:** Sweet-Talking Grandma
Champagne	**(pronounced sham păn).** She's always ready to congratulate success! **Persona:** Celebration Grandma **Fun Fact:** It is illegal for an American winery to create a new wine label using the word "Champagne."
Cher	**(pronounced shĕr).** 1. She is someone who is dear to her family and friends. 2. A superstar with a strong voice and outrageous costumes. **Persona:** Flamboyant Grandma

Grandma Story

Growing up, one woman was affectionately called Chickie because of her golden hair and energetic personality. So she declared that *Chickie* would be her Grandma name, too.

Chickie	**(pronounced chik-ē).** In a word, "hot-stuff!" Tight white jeans still look good on Chickie! **Persona:** One-Good-Looking Grandma
Chip	**(pronounced chip).** Willing to "chip in" when asked. **Persona:** Pinch-Hit Grandma
Cici	**(pronounced sē-sē).** Flirty and entertaining, Cici loves to throw a party. Hugs and kisses abound when you are with Cici! **Persona:** Wet-Kisses Grandma
Cissy	**(pronounced sĭs-ē).** Can be a "sissy" when things do not go her way. **Persona:** Grouchy Grandma

Clay	**(pronounced klā).** Lives a simple, somewhat boring life. **Persona:** Down-to-Earth Grandma
Clorox	**(pronounced klō r äks).** Grandkids could actually eat right off her kitchen floor. **Persona:** Clean-as-a-Whistle Grandma
Coco	**(pronounced kō-kō).** Has great taste and impeccable clothes. **Persona:** Sophisticated French Grandma **Fun Fact:** Famous fashion designer Coco Chanel was born Gabrielle Chanel. Coco was her name during her brief career as a cabaret singer. She never married.
Contessa	**(pronounced kŏn-tĕss-ä).** Literal Italian translation, "Italian Countess." **Persona:** Eccentric-Self-Promoting Grandma **Fun Fact:** Countess di Castiglione, better known as La Castiglione, was an Italian courtesan who achieved notoriety as a mistress of Emperor Napoleon III of France.

Coochee	**(pronounced kōō-chē).** When she tickles her grandchildren, she says, "Coochee-coo." **Persona:** Silly Grandma
Cookie	**(pronounced kōō-kē).** She's one tough cookie. **Persona:** Nothing-Can-Make-Her-Crumble Grandma
Cosmo	**(pronounced kāz mō).** She enjoys "girly" drinks. **Persona:** Fancy-Drinker Grandma
Cupid	**(pronounced kōō pid).** Hit the jackpot with husband #3. **Persona:** Love-Struck Grandma
Cuppa	**(pronounced kup pä).** Always invites you in for a "cuppa tea." **Persona:** Coffee-Shop-Tea-Bag-Swiping Grandma

Daisy

(pronounced dā zē). She brings feelings of goodness and purity.
Persona: Garden Grandma

DaMa

(pronounced dä-mä). With her long leather coats and overstuffed purses, you cannot miss DaMa.
Persona: American-Gangster Grandma

Dame

(pronounced dām). 1. A woman of rank and authority. 2. She is one grand broad.
Persona: Noble-and-Fiercely-Loyal Grandma
Fun Fact: The title of Dame is the female equivalent of Knighthood in the British honors system. In 1999, Queen Elizabeth II made Actress Elizabeth Taylor a Dame.

Dapper

(pronounced dap-er). She is super stylish and trendy.
Persona: Dressy Grandma

Anna Jarvis, the "Mother" of Mother's Day, remained unmarried and childless. Yet she made sure all mothers were honored. In 1914, President Woodrow Wilson made *Mother's Day* an official holiday.

Dede	**(pronounced dē-dē).** Tall, thin, and tan. She wears extra-large glasses with brightly colored frames and lenses. **Persona:** Fashionista Grandma
DeDoma	**(pronounced dā doma).** Bull-riding is her hobby. **Persona:** Rodeo Grandma **Fun Fact:** The sport of rodeo evolved from the Prescott Rodeo held in Prescott, AZ, on July 4th, 1888.
Deli	**(pronounced dĕl-ē).** Deli is short for "Delicatessen." **Persona:** Hot-and-Spicy Grandma

Dida	**(pronounced dē dä).** Obsessed with Bollywood movie stars. **Persona:** Bollywood Grandma **Fun Fact:** Bollywood, the Hindi film industry, is one of the largest centers of film production in the world.
Digital	**(pronounced dĭj i tel).** Social media is her jam. **Persona:** Fast-Typing Grandma **Fun Fact:** Grace Hopper was a U.S. Navy Rear Admiral and is considered the first influential woman in the field of computer programming.
Ditti	**(pronounced dĭt-tē).** Super organized, she is ready to run any fundraising event or community program. **Persona:** Give-Me-All-Your-Money Fundraiser Grandma
Diva	**(pronounced dē-vä).** Diva never leaves home without an escort. **Persona:** Hollywood-Socialite Grandma
Dodo	**(pronounced dō-dō).** She is not at her best first thing in the morning. **Persona:** Need-My-Morning-Coffee Grandma

Actress Joan Collins is *Dodo*.

Doggie	**(pronounced dô gē).** Nothing goes to waste with Doggie. **Persona:** Doggie-Bag Grandma
Doe	**(pronounced dō).** Her kind eyes adore her husband, Buck, and grandchildren. **Persona:** Hiking-and-Camping Grandma
Dolce	**(pronounced dōl se).** She moves swiftly and softly. **Persona:** Soft-Footed Grandma
Dolly	**(pronounced dŏl-ē).** Think *Hello Dolly*. She is a woman with her nose in everyone's business trying to make the world a better place. **Persona:** Life-is-a-Cabaret Grandma
Dove	**(pronounced duv).** An advocate of talks to end family feuds. **Persona:** Peace-Maker Grandma
Dozer	**(pronounced dō-zer).** She's very opinionated. **Persona:** Bull-Dozer Grandma

Drama	**(pronounced drä-mä).** Whether she is on stage or off, there is always drama. **Persona:** Broadway-Musical Grandma
Dreamy	**(pronounced drē mē).** You can often find her daydreaming. **Persona:** Head-in-the-Clouds Grandma
Duchess	**(pronounced dŭch-ĭs).** Her exact age is completely unknown. **Persona:** Royalty-Wanna-Be Grandma
Ducky	**(pronounced duk-ē).** Anyone's negativity rolls right off her back. **Persona:** Everything-Will-Be-All-Right Grandma

Egge	**(pronounced ĕg-ē).** She doesn't like the spotlight. **Persona:** Shy Grandma

Eleanor	**(pronounced əl-ë-nôr).** Eleanor is of Greek and French origins meaning "light-hearted; shining light." **Persona:** Carefree Grandma **Fun Fact:** Former First Lady Eleanor Roosevelt was known as "Grand-Mère."
Elisi	**(pronounced əl-lē-sē).** She still wears her chestnut-colored hair straight and to her waist. **Persona:** Native American Grandma
Enin	**(pronounced en in).** Can be eruptive at times. **Persona:** Volcanic Grandma **Fun Fact:** Indonesia has the largest number of active volcanoes.
Estée	**(pronounced əs-të).** Literally translated from French as "this grandmother is a star." **Persona:** Shining-Bright French Grandma
Evie	**(pronounced ē-vē).** She is a well-off woman who uses her advantages to provide for others. **Persona:** Silver-Spoon Grandma

Celebrity Grandma Story

Evelyn Lauder is the daughter-in-law of makeup empire co-founder Estée Lauder. Evelyn's grandchildren call her Evie. *Evie* created the Breast Cancer Research Fund in 1993.

Fancy	**(pronounced făn-sē).** 1. Superior grade. 2. Her afternoon teatime ritual is a cup of Darjeeling and croissants. **Persona:** Daily-Rituals-Are-Important Grandma
Fanny	**(pronounced făn-nē).** Fanny is one practical grandma. She still sports her circa 1985 fanny pack daily, so she is ready for any emergency. **Persona:** Function-over-Fashion Grandma
Farmor	**(pronounced fär-môr).** Famous for her delicious Swedish meatballs. **Persona:** Mini-Meatball Swedish Grandma

Fifi	**(pronounced fē-fē).** She is never short on advice. **Persona:** Blabber-Mouth Grandma
Flemy	**(pronounced flə-mē).** Her one and only annoying habit is that she constantly clears her throat. **Persona:** All-Stuffed-Up Grandma
Foxy	**(pronounced fŏks-sē).** 1. Cunningly shrewd; physically attractive. 2. Very comfortable in her own skin, but completely untrustworthy. **Persona:** Foxy-Lady Grandma
Frannie	**(pronounced fră-nē).** Loves to tell tall tales and be the center of attention. **Persona:** Stretching-the-Truth-Just-a-Bit Grandma
Fufoo	**(pronounced fōō-fōō).** She is not everyone's cup of tea. **Persona:** High-and-Mighty Grandma

G

(pronounced jē). "G" is a late bloomer feminist who likes to attend rallies, marches, and protests.
Persona: Feminist Grandma

Gabby

(pronounced gă-bē). Inclined to talk too much.
Persona: Chatty Grandma

Gada

(pronounced gä-dä). Likes to have structured, calm time with her grandkids. That means no amusement or water park trips with Gada.
Persona: Stiff-as-a-Board Grandma

Gaga

(pronounced gä-gä). 1. Crazy, foolish. 2. Not afraid to wield her cane at any adult or small child.
Persona: Aggressive Grandma

The month of August has the most births.
February has the least.

FUN FACT

Gaia	**(pronounced jē-ä).** Greek goddess of the Earth. **Persona:** Mother-Nature Grandma
Galini	**(pronounced gă-lē-nē).** Galini is all about living life with flair and roaming to far-off places of the world. Her husbands can rarely keep up with her. **Persona:** Worldly Grandma
Gam	**(pronounced găm).** Longtime soap opera devotee. **Persona:** Daytime TV Grandma

Grandma Story

One grandmother-to-be joked she was actually "*G.G.*" = God's Girlfriend.

Gamcha	**(pronounced găm-chă).** Some days she just cannot be found. **Persona:** Wandering Grandma
Gamma	**(pronounced găm-ma).** Her stern looks convey all. **Persona:** Woman-of-Few-Words Grandma

Gammlemor	**(pronounced găm-lĕ-mōr).** Sophisticated and well-heeled, she expects good behavior at all times. Pressed pantsuits are a favorite of Gammlemor. **Persona:** Well-Bred Norwegian Grandma
Gamommie	**(pronounced găm-mŏm-ē).** On the weekends, Gamommie can be found running local 5K road races. **Persona:** Exercise-Fanatic Grandma
Gammy	**(pronounced găm-mē).** 1. Showing resolute spirit: plucky. 2. Her single strand of pearls and matching earrings belie her wild past. **Persona:** American-Political-Family Grandma
Gammy-Goose	**(pronounced găm-mē-gōōs).** White-haired and wild. Goose comes and goes as she pleases. **Persona:** As-the-Wind-Blows Grandma

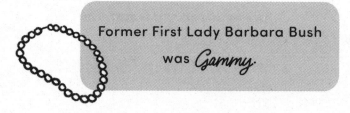

Former First Lady Barbara Bush was *Gammy.*

Gams	**(pronounced găms).** Gams has great legs. **Persona:** Rockette Grandma
Gayga	**(pronounced gā-gă).** Her direct involvement with her grandchildren is sending timely birthday presents. **Persona:** Standoffish Grandma
Gee	**(pronounced jē).** A happy name for a happy person. **Persona:** Cheerful Grandma
Gibber	**(pronounced jib-er).** She sometimes speaks so rapidly, it's unintelligible. **Persona:** Can't-Stop-Talking Grandma
Giga	**(pronounced gig-ä).** She's one-in-a-billion. **Persona:** Billion-Dollar Grandma
Giget	**(pronounced gi-jət).** Small in stature with big ideas; hangs with the boys. **Persona:** Tomboyish Grandma
Giggles	**(pronounced gig-els).** Her giggly personality belies occasional nervousness. **Persona:** Giggly Grandma

Giggy	**(pronounced jig-gē).** Always ready to "get down!" **Persona:** With-It Grandma
Gigi	**(pronounced jē-jē).** Gigi never forgets to put on her makeup, or at least lipstick, before leaving the house. **Persona:** Everybody-Loves Grandma
Gigia	**(pronounced j-jē-ä).** Gigia is mysterious and very independent. **Persona:** Glorious Greek Grandma
Gimme	**(pronounced gim-mē).** Always willing to take the grandkids. **Persona:** Can't-Get-Enough Grandma

Celebrity Grandma Story

Chef Paula Deen was a guest on *The Today Show* with Kathie Lee and Hoda Kotb. Hoda asked Paula, "What does your grandson call you?" Paula replied, "Well, there was a lot of arguing about that. My son suggested 'Big Mama.' I told him if he called me Big Mama, I was going to kick his big ass right out of my will!" Chef Paula Deen is *Ginny*.

Ginger	**(pronounced jin-jər).** Has light reddish-yellow or orange-brown color hair and can "ginger" up any situation. **Persona:** Spicy Grandma
Ginny	**(pronounced jĭn-nē).** A down-to-earth woman made from scratch. **Persona:** Worked-My-Way-up-the-Hard-Way Grandma
Girdle	**(pronounced gurd-l).** Doesn't like jiggles or wiggles. **Persona:** Old-Fashioned Grandma **Fun Fact:** A girdle is essentially a partial corset claiming to improve posture, show off assets, and hide "liabilities!"
Glitter	**(pronounced glid-er).** Her sparkly personality can sometimes be blinding. **Persona:** Exuberant Grandma
Glover	**(pronounced gl-ovər).** Grandma + Lover. **Persona:** Amorous Grandma

Glamma	**(pronounced glăm-mä).** Glamma is glamorous and stylish. She looks younger than her years. **Persona:** Hollywood Grandma **Fun Fact:** Actress Goldie Hawn goes by Glamma.
Glam Mom	**(pronounced glăm-mom).** Is she the mom or grandma? **Persona:** Turned-Back-Time Grandma
G-Ma	**(pronounced jē-mä).** A contemporary version of Grandma, G-Ma is confident and street smart. There is no "pulling the wool" over G-Ma's eyes! **Persona:** Street-Smart Grandma
G-Mama	**(pronounced jē-mä-mä).** Is adamant about using the salutation Ms. not Mrs. She has been a feminist all her life. **Persona:** Socially-Progressive Grandma
G-Mom	**(pronounced jē-mŏm).** Loves to crochet while watching those evening reality shows. **Persona:** Evening-Couch-Potato Grandma

Goddess	**(pronounced gŏd-ĭs).** A woman of exceptional beauty and charm. She believes that being a woman is cool… you've got all the power. **Persona:** I-Am-Woman-Hear-Me-Roar Grandma
Go-Go	**(pronounced gō-gō).** Just watch her go-go-go! **Persona:** Multitasking Grandma
Golda	**(pronounced gŏl-dä).** Strong-willed, straight-talking, grey-bunned grandma. **Persona:** Visionary Grandma **Fun Fact:** Golda Meir is considered to be the "Grandmother of the Jewish people."
Golly	**(pronounced gŏl-ē).** She is someone who does not take herself too seriously. **Persona:** Joyful Grandma
Gommy	**(pronounced gŏm-mē).** She is all the best of Mommy! **Persona:** Superlative Grandma
Goobie	**(pronounced goo-bē).** She's always there for you. **Persona:** Stuck-on-You Grandma

NYC real estate mogul Barbara Corcoran is *Glamma*

Goose	**(pronounced gōōs).** Fluffy pancakes with powdered sugar are her signature breakfast. She's up before the crack of dawn. **Persona:** Early-Bird-Gets-the-Worm Grandma
Gra	**(pronounced grä).** She can be tough and firm, but her grandchildren make her all soft and cuddly. **Persona:** Old-Softy Grandma
Grady	**(pronounced grä-dē).** A party Grandmother! It quickly becomes "5:00 PM somewhere" when you are with her. **Persona:** Happy-Hour Grandma
Gram	**(pronounced grăm).** Gram's candy drawer is just at the right height, filled with every kind of forbidden sweet treat! **Persona:** All-American Grandma
Grama	**(pronounced grăm-mə).** Her favorite book is *Heloise Household Hints*. **Persona:** Neat-and-Tidy Grandma

Gramarama	**(pronounced grăm-ă-rămă).** She has a great laugh—her whole body shakes when she laughs. **Persona:** Giggling Grandma
Grambo	**(pronounced gram-bō).** She has no problem scooping up the grandkids! **Persona:** Rambo Grandma
Grammers	**(pronounced gram-ərs).** She's big on grammar—always ready to correct! **Persona:** Scholarly Grandma
Grammy	**(pronounced grăm-mē).** Napping on Grammy's needlepoint pillows will certainly leave an impression. **Persona:** American-Sampler Grandma
Gramsy	**(pronounced grăm-sē).** Whimsical chicken paraphernalia decorate her home. **Persona:** Quirky Grandma

Create your own unique grandma name by merging "Gran" with your name.

Gran + Nancy = Grancy
Gran + Angela = Grangela

Grand	**(pronounced grănd).** She may not be large, but she sure is in charge! **Persona:** Gives-the-Orders Grandma **Fun Fact:** Jackie Kennedy Onassis was Grand Jackie.
Grand Dame	**(pronounced grănd-dām).** No other qualities are more important to her than lineage and pedigree. **Persona:** Snobby Grandma
Grand DiggityDog	**(pronounced grănd-dĭg-ĭtē-dôg).** Stray animals know just where to go! **Persona:** Animal-Lover Grandma
Grand Maman	**(pronounced grănd´memä).** Attends Cannes every year. **Persona:** Film-Buff Grandma **Fun Fact:** France has the most Michelin Starred restaurants with 600 in total.
Grand Mum	**(pronounced grănd-mum).** Neighbors say her Irish soda bread is out of this world. **Persona:** Irish-Baking Grandma

Former Supreme Court Justice
Sandra Day O'Connor was *Grandma*.

Former First Lady Jackie Kennedy was *Grand Jackie.*

Grande	**(pronounced grănd-dē).** Her laugh is exuberant and infectious. **Persona:** Most-High Grandma
Grandma	**(pronounced grănd´mă).** Affectionate and kind. She cannot resist tickling and squeezing her grandkids when she sees them. **Persona:** The-Best-Kind-of Grandma
Grandma Great	**(pronounced grănd-mă-grāt).** Oriental rugs and large oil paintings accent her large Victorian home. **Persona:** Victorian-Era Grandma
Grandma Nana	**(pronounced grăndmă nănä).** She's the top dog grandma. **Persona:** Double-Moniker Grandma
Grandmama	**(pronounced grănd-mă-mä).** She refers often to her life in the old country. **Persona:** Nostalgic Grandma **Fun Fact:** Grandmama was the grandmother in the 1960s TV show, *The Addams Family.* A.k.a., Granny Frump.

GrandMamy	**(pronounced grănd-mă-mee).** Has taken care of so many children she has lost count. **Persona:** Surrogate-Mom Grandma
Grandmaw	**(pronounced grănd-mô).** Even with her thick southern drawl, her words are never mistaken by anyone. **Persona:** Always-Has-Your-Back Grandma
Grand-Mère	**(pronounced grănd-měr).** Never goes anywhere without her tiny, well-groomed Chihuahua. **Persona:** City-of-Love French Grandma
Grandmissy	**(pronounced grănd-mis-ē).** Voted most popular girl in high school. **Persona:** Prom-Queen Grandma
Grandmom	**(pronounced grănd-mŏm).** Her "Don't mess with Grandma" bumper sticker says it all. **Persona:** Military Grandma

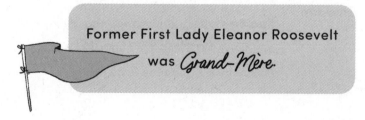

Former First Lady Eleanor Roosevelt was *Grand-Mère.*

Grandmuck	**(pronounced grănd-muk).** Lives on a backroad, swampy property. **Persona:** Sporadic-Electricity Grandma
Grandnan	**(pronounced grănd-nan).** She never scolds, just wrings her hands on her apron. **Persona:** Old-Fashioned Grandma
Grandnana	**(pronounced grănd-nă-nə).** She still likes to ride her horses first thing in the morning. **Persona:** Old-Money Grandma
GranGram	**(pronounced grăn-grăm).** Everyone is so proud that GranGram wins the prized pie contest every year at the local fair! **Persona:** Loves-to-Bake Grandma
GranGran	**(pronounced grăn-grăn).** She never flinches when filleting fish freshly caught by her grandkids. **Persona:** Cape-Cod Grandma
Granky	**(pronounced grănkē).** Easily irritated by little ones. **Persona:** Cranky Grandma

Granma	**(pronounced grăn-mă).** Never lets little ones go outside or go to bed with wet hair. **Persona:** Old-Wives-Tales Grandma

Granny Clampett was the redneck grandmother on the 1960s hit TV show *The Beverly Hillbillies.*

FUN FACT

Granmomma	**(pronounced grăn-mŏm-mä).** Granmomma was the first of her girlfriends to earn an athletic varsity letter jacket in high school. **Persona:** Sporty Grandma
Granna	**(pronounced grăn-nä).** Too many good features to name. Combo name of Grandma and Nana. **Persona:** She's-the-Best-of-Both-Names Grandma
Granno	**(pronounced grăn-no).** Enjoys all of her grandchildren's performances. **Persona:** My-Grandchild-Is-#1 Grandma

Granny	**(pronounced grăn-nē).** An authentic, veritable delight. On any given day, you might find Granny sitting on her porch swing with a shotgun in her hands. **Persona:** Grits-and-Gravy Grandma
Grannyma	**(pronounced grăn-nē-mă).** Grannyma's worn-out blue jean overalls are relics, but they look perfect on her. **Persona:** Southern Grandma
Grannymama	**(pronounced grăn-nē-mă-mä).** No one can handle a John Deere tractor like Grannymama. **Persona:** Down-on-the-Farm Grandma
Granzilla	**(pronounced grăn-zil-ä).** Typically reserved for mothers-in-law; monster grandmother. **Persona:** Scary Grandma

President Franklin Delano Roosevelt's mother, Sara Delano Roosevelt, was known as *Granny*.

Gree-Gree	**(pronounced grē-grē).** Gree-Gree lives high up on a hill, making frequent family visitors infrequent. She likes it that way. **Persona:** Solitary Grandma
Gremmon	**(pronounced grə-mŏn).** Fancy hats and ladies' luncheons at the club are her pastime favorites. **Persona:** Protestant Grandma
Grenade	**(pronounced grə-nād).** Don't speak ill of her grandchildren. **Persona:** Ready-to-Blow Grandma
Greta	**(pronounced gret-ä).** Greta has a sunny and light personality. **Persona:** Always-Shining Grandma **Fun Fact:** Greta Garbo was the beautiful 1920s & 1930s Swedish American actress.
Grootmoeder	**(pronounced grōōt-moder).** At times, she can be full of hot air. **Persona:** Wind-Powered Dutch Grandma
Grossmutter	**(pronounced grōs-mut-ər).** Neat, tidy, and never "colors outside the lines" is Grossmutter. **Persona:** Stern German Grandma

Gua-ma	**(pronounced gwä-mä).** No need for cooking; street food is abundant. **Persona:** Night-Shopping Twaiwanese Grandma
Gubbe	**(pronounced gub-bē).** Great-Grandma Bubbe a.k.a. Gubbe. **Persona:** Mother of Bubbe
Guid Mathair	**(pronounced goo-id matir).** You can often find her red-in-the-face. **Persona:** Bagpipe-Playing Scottish Grandma
Gumma	**(pronounced gum-mä).** Gummas have a firm, neurotic center. There is no telling in what sort of mood she will be. **Persona:** Psycho Not-Here-to-Impress-Anyone Grandma

In the U.S., approximately 10,267 babies are born every day! That's over 3 million babies every year! The number of births for the United States in 2021 was 3,659,289. That's approximately 10,025 babies born every day!

FUN FACT

Happy	**(pronounced hăp-ē).** She likes to say, "A heart that loves is always young." **Persona:** Old-Greek-Saying Grandma
Halmoni	**(pronounced hăl-mōnē).** Glowing skin Grandma. **Persona:** Korean-Cosmetics Grandma
Halo	**(pronounced hā-lō).** Predisposition to admire (a.k.a. exaggerate) her grandchildren's feats. **Persona:** Halo-Effect Grandma
Hamma	**(pronounced hăm-mə).** Classic-looking Grandma. **Persona:** Handsome Grandma
Handsy	**(pronounced hănd-sē).** Actively participates in grandchildren rearing. **Persona:** Hands-on Grandma
Handy	**(pronounced hăn-dē).** Can solve any problem. **Persona:** Always-Needed Grandma

Heiress	**(pronounced her-əs).** Will inherit considerable wealth. **Persona:** Trust-Fund Grandma
Highness	**(pronounced hī-nes).** Expects obedience from grandkids. **Persona:** Has-Friends-in-High-Places Grandma
Hillary	**(pronounced hĭl-er-ē).** She enjoys debating about international issues. **Persona:** Political Grandma
Hippy	**(pronounced hĭp-ē).** Hippy is very cool and likes wearing long, flowing skirts and hemp necklaces. **Persona:** Woodstock Grandma
Homey	**(pronounced ho-mē).** Not to be confused with Homely. She's mostly a homebody. **Persona:** Rarely-Ventures-Outside Grandma
Honey	**(pronounced hŭn-ē).** Honey is as sweet as her name. She remembers those long-forgotten Sunday drives. **Persona:** American-Nostalgia Grandma **Fun Fact:** Honey bees are one of the social bees that produce honey.

Hopie	**(pronounced hō-pē).** Believes she is the #1 Grandma. **Persona:** Delusional Grandma
Huggie	**(pronounced hŭg-ē).** She is tough, dry, and dependable. **Persona:** Waterproof Grandma
Hussy	**(pronounced hŭs-ē).** Hussy is slightly immoral, very brazen, and just a bit mischievous. **Persona:** Oh-No-Here-She-Comes Grandma

Insta-Gram	**(pronounced insta-grăm).** Tech-savvy grandma who's constantly posting grandkids' pictures on social media. **Persona:** Tech-Savvy Grandma
Isis	**(pronounced ī-sis).** Adores her "goddess-like" girlfriends. **Persona:** Egyptian-Goddess Grandma **Fun Fact:** Isis was the Egyptian goddess of fertility and known as the goddess of Motherhood.

Jadda	**(pronounced jā-dä).** She likes to say, "Every age has its book." **Persona:** Old-Arabic-Saying Grandma
Jammie	**(pronounced jăm-ē).** You never get too old for a sleepover at Jammie's. **Persona:** Flannel-Nightgown Grandma
Jazzy	**(pronounced jăzz-ē).** She loves listening to her jazz radio station. **Persona:** Dancing-in-the-Kitchen Grandma
Jewel	**(pronounced joo-el).** She loves her diamonds and jewels. **Persona:** Sparkly Grandma
JinJin	**(pronounced jĭn-jĭn).** A self-proclaimed artist. She enjoys drawing and painting with her grandchildren. **Persona:** Artistic Grandma
Jiggy	**(pronounced jĭg-ē).** Look out for flying arms and legs when Jiggy hits the dance floor. **Persona:** Two-Left-Feet Grandma

The famous 1930s–1950s film actress Joan Crawford was known as

JuJu	**(pronounced jū-jū).** She has supernatural powers. **Persona:** West-African Grandma
June	**(pronounced jūn).** June likes to sleep in on most days. **Persona:** Summer-Vacation Grandma
Juno	**(pronounced jūn-ō).** Juno was the Queen of the Gods. **Persona:** Roman-Goddess Grandma **Fun Fact:** Her symbol is the peacock. Juno's husband is Jupiter, king of the gods.

K

Kitty	**(pronounced kit-tē).** Husband #4 thinks she is beautiful. **Persona:** Matrimonial Grandma

Kryptonite	**(pronounced krip-tō-nīt).** She has been working out faithfully with her sexy, young personal trainer. **Persona:** Longtime-YMCA-Member Grandma
Kupuna	**(pronounced kä-pōō-nə).** A former Hawaiian Airlines stewardess who placed leis on de-planing passengers. **Persona:** Beautiful Hawaiian Grandma

Princes William and Harry called their Grandma, Queen Elizabeth II, *Granny.*

L

Lady	**(pronounced lā-dē).** She is a well-mannered woman with high standards. An imported, one-of-a-kind, chic handbag can always be found dangling from her arm. **Persona:** American-Royalty Grandma
Laffy	**(pronounced laf-fē).** Always ready with a corny joke. **Persona:** Humorous Grandma

Lala	**(pronounced lä-lä).** She still sneaks that daily cigarette. **Persona:** Where-Did-She-Go-Now Grandma
Lala Manita	**(pronounced lä-lä mä nē tä).** Loves her ruffled red and black tango-dancing costume. **Persona:** Flamenco-Dancing Grandma **Fun Fact:** The five most popular Flamenco dances are: Tango, Sevillanas, Bulerias, Alegrias, and Fandango.
Lalo	**(pronounced lä-lō).** She radiates positive energy. **Persona:** Laughter-Is-the-Best-Medicine
Lela	**(pronounced lā-lä).** She has never veered from her morning ritual: full body stretch, ten toe touches, brush hair, moisturize, and then make strong coffee. **Persona:** Ritualistic Grandma
LiLi	**(pronounced lē-lē).** LiLi usually has something up her sleeve. It is an unpredictable adventure with Lili. **Persona:** Dependable-But-Unpredictable Grandma

Actress Blythe Danner
(Gwyneth Paltrow's mom) is *Lolo*.

Lilly	**(pronounced lĭl-ē).** Headbands keep her hair neat and tidy. **Persona:** Pure-and-Refined Grandma **Fun Fact:** The lily flower symbolizes purity and beauty.
Lola	**(pronounced lō-lä).** The name Lola conjures up sultry images and colorful clothes. Weekly Senior Salsa dancing keeps her in shape. **Persona:** Disco Spanish Grandma
Lolly	**(pronounced lŏl-ē).** With her crisp, white tennis outfit and hair perfectly twisted into a bun, she can always be spotted on the court. **Persona:** Upper-Class Grandma **Fun Fact:** American Journalist Leslie Stahl is Lolly.
Love	**(pronounced lŭv).** Watch out for those great, big, red lipstick kisses. **Persona:** Glamour Grandma

Lovey	**(pronounced lŭv-ē).** Hates to miss out on any event during the social season. She is more comfortable socializing with those on the social register. **Persona:** Socially-Prominent Grandma **Fun Fact:** Mrs. Lovey Howell was the rich, spoiled socialite on the 1960s comedy TV show, *Gilligan's Island*.
Lucky	**(pronounced lŭk-ē).** "Diligence is the mother of good luck."—Benjamin Franklin. **Persona:** Find-a-Penny-Pick-It-Up Grandma
Lulu	**(pronounced lōō-lōō).** Believes her grandchildren are angels on Earth. **Persona:** Heavenly Grandma

> "A house needs a grandmother in it."
>
> *—Louisa May Alcott, author*

Ma	**(pronounced mä).** Usually can be found meddling in someone's affairs. **Persona:** Way-Too-Involved Grandma
Madonna	**(pronounced mä-don-nä).** Like a virgin? **Persona:** Holy-Roller Grandma
Mae	**(pronounced mä).** A life-long librarian who would not think of reading anything but classic literature to her grandkids. **Persona:** Literary Grandma
Maga	**(pronounced mä-gä).** Habit of purchasing unnecessary tchotchkes for her grandchildren and daughters-in-law. **Persona:** Saturday-Yard-Sales Grandma
Majesty	**(pronounced mə-jes-tē).** 1. State of being impressive or dignified. 2. She is vain and unapproachable. **Persona:** Nose-in-the-Air Grandma
Maia	**(pronounced mī-ə).** Literally translated from Greek, "Good Mother." **Persona:** Good Greek Grandma

Maimeó	**(pronounced mä-mēō).** Excellent hidden treasure shopper. **Persona:** Irish Leprechaun Grandma
Main Ma	**(pronounced män mä).** She is undoubtably in charge. **Persona:** Matriarch Grandma
Makhulu	**(pronounced mak-ōō-lōō).** Stray cats know where to go. **Persona:** Safari-Going Grandma
Mama	**(pronounced mä-mä).** She has the magic of maternal family leadership (or is it dictatorship?). **Persona:** Controlling Grandma
Mama Joon	**(pronounced mä-mä-joon).** Literal Persian translation, "mama dear." **Persona:** Soulful Farsi Grandma
Mamie	**(pronounced mä-mē).** Still prefers girdles. **Persona:** Old-Fashioned-Contraption Grandma

Actor Matthew McConaughey's mother is *MaMac.*

MaMoo	**(pronounced mä-mōō).** MaMoo regularly trolls Marshalls for bargains. Hard-to-find household items and trinkets are her specialty. A bargain is a bargain! **Persona:** American-Spender Grandma
Mamy	**(pronounced mä mē).** Makes world-famous waffles. **Persona:** Belgian Grandma
Manama	**(pronounced mă-nă-mă).** Manama is like a Mexican jumping bean—she just can't sit still. **Persona:** Jumpy Mexican Grandma
Manita	**(pronounced măn-ē-tă).** Spanish term of endearment for Mother. A hot bowl of Manita's homemade soup can make everything all right. **Persona:** Special Spanish Grandma
Manny	**(pronounced măn-ē).** Menswear is what she wears. **Persona:** She-Wears-the-Pants Grandma

Marme	**(pronounced mär-mē).** Think Little Women. She is someone with kind words and heartfelt empathy for everyone she meets. **Persona:** Old-Fashioned-Hard-Working Grandma
Martha	**(pronounced măr-thă).** One 99-year-old great-grandmother felt that she clearly was not old enough to be called Grandma, so they called her Martha. **Persona:** Don't-Mess-with Grandma
Maw-Maw	**(pronounced mô-mô).** Would not be caught without her skin-colored pantyhose. **Persona:** Good-Southern-Manners Grandma
May	**(pronounced mā).** Has been dutifully serving for years on the local Women's and Garden Club boards. **Persona:** American-Civic-Duty Grandma
Medley	**(pronounced med-lē).** Potluck dinners are her specialty. **Persona:** BYO Grandma

Medusa	**(pronounced mĭ dusä).** Her looks could turn you to stone. **Persona:** Dreadlocks Grandma
MeMa	**(pronounced mē-mä).** Be cautious when approaching MeMa about the family history. Some parts of family history are "not to be discussed." **Persona:** This-Doesn't-Leave-the-Table Grandma
MeMaw	**(pronounced mē-mô).** She is not one to back down from a fight, but diplomatic in her discussions. You can always count on MeeMaw to "have your back." **Persona:** Old-Faithful-and-Dependable Grandma

Country singer Naomi Judd was *Mamaw*.

MeMo	**(pronounced mē-mō).** Can be a worrier, but will put on a happy face to disguise her feelings. **Persona:** Ulcer Grandma

MeMom	**(pronounced mē-mŏm).** Unflappable and dependable. She is a Grandma who you can confide in without judgment. **Persona:** Mum's-the-Word Grandma
Merry	**(pronounced me-rē).** Winter holidays and traditions are her favorite. **Persona:** Festive Grandma
Mica	**(pronounced mī-kä).** Rules and order, clearly defined by Mica, must be adhered to upon entering her home. **Persona:** My-Way-or-the-Highway Serbian Grandma
Midi	**(pronounced mid-ē).** Music is constantly playing throughout her entire home. **Persona:** Sound System Grandma **Fun Fact:** MIDI is short for Musical Instrument Digital Interface.
MILe	**(pronounced mil-ē).** Not ready for the next phase of life. **Persona:** Can't-Accept-the-Truth Grandma **Fun Fact:** MIL is short for Mother-In-Law.

Milky	**(pronounced mil kē).** Has beautiful milky skin. **Persona:** Oil-of-Olay Grandma
MILma	**(pronounced mil-mä).** Loves both roles—MIL and Grandma! **Persona:** Son-Chose-Well Grandma
Mim	**(pronounced mĭm).** Super sophisticated with flawless taste. She enjoys frequenting local art galleries, theaters, and museums with her grandkids. **Persona:** Well-Traveled Grandma
Mimi	**(pronounced mĭm-ē or mē-mē).** She is one smart, savvy, hip grandmother. **Persona:** Totally-With-It Grandma

"Painting's not important. The important thing is that we keep busy."

—Grandma Moses, American folk artist

Mimmé	**(pronounced mĭm-mā).** Of Portuguese descent, she is a woman who works hard at all that she does but sets special time aside for family. She avails herself to everyone, but also takes care of herself. **Persona:** Dedicated Portuguese Grandma
Moma	**(pronounced mŏm-mə).** Her car proudly displays bumper stickers from every grandchild's college! **Persona:** College-Fund Grandma
Momanana	**(pronounced mŏm-ä-nă-nä).** It is an anagram, "A Nana Mom." **Persona:** Scrabble-Playing Grandma
Momma	**(pronounced mŏm-mä).** A career woman who relies on her slow cooker every day. **Persona:** Working-Girl Grandma
Momme	**(pronounced mŏm-may).** Even when the wind blows, Momme's hair stays in place! **Persona:** Hair-Spray Grandma

| **Mommia** | **(pronounced mŏm-mīā).** Being of Italian heritage.
Persona: Italian Grandma |

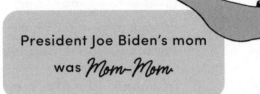

President Joe Biden's mom was *Mom-Mom*.

Mom-Mom	**(pronounced mŏm-mŏm).** She is twice the fun! **Persona:** Double-Trouble Grandma
MoMo	**(pronounced mō-mō).** She is a former piano teacher who loves playing the piano for her grandchildren. **Persona:** Musical Grandma
Moo	**(pronounced mōō).** Moo carries crackling, plastic-wrapped candy in her jacket pockets. **Persona:** Sweet-Tooth Grandma
MopMop	**(pronounced mŏp-mŏp).** Speaks up regularly at the monthly town hall meetings. **Persona:** Mayor Grandma

MoreNana	**(pronounced môr-na-nä).** What grandchild would not want more of Nana? **Persona:** American Grandma
Mormor	**(pronounced môr-môr).** Literal Swedish translation, "Mother's Mother." **Persona:** Swedish Grandma
MoxieMom	**(pronounced mŏks-ē-mŏm).** She has a unique, although somewhat bitter, flavor to her. **Persona:** She-Can-Hit-a-Nerve Grandma
Mum	**(pronounced mŭm).** You will always find Mum dressed properly with matching shoes, pocketbook, and hat. **Persona:** British Grandma

National Grandparents Day is celebrated the first Sunday after Labor Day annually!

Mummi	**(pronounced mōō-mē).** She likes to say, "A bird in the hand is worth ten in the bush." **Persona:** Old-Finnish-Saying Grandma

Mummica	**(pronounced mŭm-mī-kā).** Meat and potatoes are staple dishes of Mummica. They just come in different dinner combinations every time. **Persona:** 1950s Grandma
Mummo	**(pronounced moo-mä).** One of the happiest people in the world. **Persona:** Finnish Grandma **Fun Fact:** Finland was crowned the happiest country in the world (2022). Denmark was second.
Mummy	**(pronounced mŭm-ē).** She would wear spandex under her bathing suit if she could. **Persona:** All-Wrapped-Up Grandma

Nai Nai

(pronounced nī-nī). She likes to say, "One generation plants the trees; another gets the shade."
Persona: Old-Chinese-Saying Grandma

Namma

(pronounced năm-mă). Loves her Florida home in the winter and her upstate New York home in the summer.
Persona: Snow-Bird Grandma

Nan

(pronounced năn). A hipper, more contemporary Nana. She still colors her hair to cover the greys.
Persona: Weekly-Beauty-Salon Grandma

Nanay

(pronounced nă-nā). When you don't know what name to choose, but you want to be referred to with respect!
Persona: High-Brow Grandma

Nana

(pronounced nă-nä). Loving, kind and generous describes Nana. She has a passion for cleaning her house and ironing everyone's clothes.
Persona: Loves-You-Unconditionally Grandma

Create your own contemporary name!

Create a new grandma name by making a diminutive of your own name:

Lisa = Lili

Denise = Didi

Susan = Susu

Nana-Grandma	**(pronounced nă-nä-grănd-mă).** She never says "No" to any grandchild's request. **Persona:** Sweetheart Grandma
Nana-New-Face	**(pronounced nă-nä new face).** Looking younger is her obsession. **Persona:** Vacations-Are-for-Recovering Grandma **Fun Fact:** Comedian Joan Rivers called herself "Nana-New-Face."
Nanamoo	**(pronounced nă-nä-mōō).** She's just so darn cute. **Persona:** Out-of-the-Ballpark Grandma **Fun Fact:** Baseball hall-of-famer Nolan Ryan's wife, Ruth, is Nanamoo.

Nanny
(pronounced nă-nē). Her beach house is located near the best clam shack ever!
Persona: Down-by-the-Bay Grandma

Famous relationship psychologist Dr. Dale Atkins is *Nana*

Nanoo
(pronounced năn-nōō). Sturdy and well-built. A wool sweater is all she needs in subzero weather.
Persona: Thick-Skinned Grandma
Fun Fact: "Nanoo Nanoo" was the salutation used by TV character Mork on the series *Mork and Mindy*. Robin Williams played Mork and Pam Dawson played Mindy.

Nauna
(pronounced nôn-nä). Dusting is her specialty— whether at her home or yours!
Persona: Got-to-Keep-Moving Italian Grandma

Nem
(pronounced něm). Little girls love playing at Nem's makeup vanity overflowing with the latest makeup products and even false eyelashes!
Persona: Makeup Grandma

Nena	**(pronounced ne-nä).** Loves bobsledding in the winter! **Persona:** Daredevil Sarajevo Grandma
Nini	**(pronounced nē-nē).** Doting, loving, and somewhat scatterbrained. **Persona:** Dizzy Grandma **Fun Fact:** When texting, NiNi is short for saying Night-Night or Good-Night.
NinnaNana	**(pronounced nĭn-ä-nă-nä).** She likes to say, "Old wine and friends improve with age." **Persona:** Old-Italian-Saying Grandma

Comedian Joan Rivers was *Nana New-Face.*

Nonna	**(pronounced nŏn-nă).** Authentic Nonnas call their homemade tomato sauce "gravy." **Persona:** Eat-Some-then-Eat-Some-More Italian Grandma **Fun Fact:** Giada De Laurentiis, famous Food Network chef, called her grandma Nonna Luna because she was the first one to show Giada the moon.

Nonnie	**(pronounced nŏn-nē).** Not as old-fashioned as Nonna, but appreciates big family dinners. Cooking is her favorite pastime. **Persona:** Always-Cooking Italian Grandma
Nonnina	**(pronounced nŏn-nină).** A petite version of traditional Nonna. When excited, she speaks in both Italian and English. **Persona:** Tiny-but-Tough Italian Grandma
Noodle	**(pronounced noo-del).** Plays and interacts with little ones effortlessly. **Persona:** Game-Playing Grandma
Nooney	**(pronounced noon-nē).** A very self-sufficient grandma who drives herself everywhere. **Persona:** Super-Independent Grandma

Actress Priscilla Presley is *Nonna*

Normy

(**pronounced nôr-mē**). She goes with the flow.

Persona: Normal Grandma

No-Show

(**pronounced nō shō**). No interest in babysitting the grandkids.

Persona: No-Show Grandma

Nouveau

(**pronounced nu-vō**). Not sure what to do now.

Persona: Newly French Grandma

NunNun

(**pronounced nun-nun**). Like a 1950s Catholic nun, she can be somewhat rigid and demanding.

Persona: Leader-of-the-Pack Grandma

Fun Fact: Mother Teresa of Calcutta was a famous nun.

Nigeria has the highest birth rate in the world.

Obaachan	**(pronounced ō-bä-chan).** She takes very small, but very quick steps. **Persona:** Light-on-Her-Feet Japanese Grandma
Obaasan	**(pronounced ō-bä-san).** Although she rarely smiles, she cares deeply for her family. **Persona:** Quiet Japanese Grandma
Oldemor	**(pronounced ōl-de-môr).** Literal Norwegian translation, "Great-Grandma." **Persona:** Norwegian Great-Grandma
Ona Great	**(pronounced ōna-grāt).** One whose grace is amazing. **Persona:** Princess Grandma
Oopsy	**(pronounced ōp-sē).** She is strangely clumsy. **Persona:** Head-in-the-Clouds Grandma
Oma	**(pronounced ō-mə).** Always ready to take off with grandkids. She is extremely proud of her heritage. **Persona:** On-the-Move German Grandma

Omina	**(pronounced ō-mēnä).** Doesn't beat-around-the-bush; she's direct and forthright. **Persona:** Petite German Grandmother
Ouma	**(pronounced ōō-mä).** She likes to say, "It is better to trust the eyes rather than the ears." **Persona:** Trust-Your-Intuition Grandma

Actor Leonardo DiCaprio's grandma was *Oma*.

Petunia	**(pronounced pə-tōōn-yä).** 1. Wide funnel-shaped spring flower. 2. Every Sunday in spring, Petunia heads to church wearing her fashionable Easter hat, fancy dress, and white gloves. **Persona:** Spring-into-Action Grandma

Picky	**(pronounced pĭk-ē).** 1. Literally translated as fussy. 2. When ordering at restaurants, she asks so many questions that it is embarrassing. **Persona:** Can't-Make-Up-Her-Mind Grandma
Plucky	**(pronounced plŭk-ē).** She is notably spirited and courageous. **Persona:** Gutsy Grandma
PoPo	**(pronounced pō-pō).** She likes to say, "Walls have ears and little pots, too." **Persona:** Old-Chinese-Saying Grandma
Pretty	**(pronounced prĭt-ē).** Loves wearing her 100% virgin-wool navy-blue peacoat with shiny brass buttons. **Persona:** Never-Goes-out-of-Style Grandma
Princess	**(pronounced prĭn-sĕs).** Expects the royal treatment. **Persona:** Crown-Wearing Grandma
Principessa	**(pronounced prĭn-sĕ-pĕs-ä).** She still has that great sparkle in her clear baby-blue eyes. **Persona:** Can-Light-up-the-Room Italian Grandma

Quacky

(pronounced kwăk-ē). Never leaves her house without "putting on" her eyelashes and eyebrows.
Persona: Vanity Grandma

Queenie

(pronounced kwēn-nē). Pedicures and manicures are a favorite weekly indulgence of Queenie.
Persona: High-Maintenance Grandma

Quirky

(pronounced kwurk-ē). She does not seek the limelight.
Persona: Do-Your-Own-Thing Grandma

Regal

(pronounced rē-gəl). Regal's skirts are hemmed precisely two inches below her kneecap.
Persona: Uptight Grandma

Renegade	**(pronounced rĕn-ĭ-gād).** Homeownership never interested Renegade…she prefers to rent so she can roam freely. **Persona:** Free-Spirit Grandma
Robo	**(pronounced rō-bō).** She is just going through the motions at this stage. **Persona:** It-Is-What-It-Is Grandma
Ruler	**(pronounced rōō-lər).** Strict and proper. **Persona:** No-Fun Grandma
Rusty	**(pronounced rŭs-tē).** Years of hoarding now limits the number of family members who can visit her. **Persona:** Gotta-Have-It Grandma

S

Sassy	**(pronounced săs-sē).** A take-charge grandma who is always full of ideas and adventure. World traveling is her specialty! **Persona:** Adventurous-and-Daring Grandma
Scooby	**(pronounced skōō-bē).** Her 1979 Chevy Impala convertible still passes inspection every year. **Persona:** Car-Aficionado Grandma
Sean-mháthair	**(pronounced shan-waw-her).** She likes to say, "A face without freckles is like a sky without stars." **Persona:** Old-Irish-Saying Grandma
Snazzy	**(pronounced snaz-ē).** 1. Attractive in a flashy or showy way. 2. She believes that dressing in animal print clothes will diffuse a hot flash. **Persona:** Flashily-Attractive Grandma
Snookie	**(pronounced snŏŏk-ē).** She is someone who rarely sleeps. You never know when Snookie might show up. **Persona:** Never-Ceases-to-Amaze Grandma

In 2022, there were over 2.5 million weddings— the most in almost 40 years!

Soba	**(pronounced so bä).** Kabuki baths are a favorite indulgence. **Persona:** Spa-Going Japanese Grandma
Star	**(pronounced stär).** The twinkle in her eyes belies fun trouble. **Persona:** Astrologer Grandma
Sugar	**(pronounced shŏŏ-gər).** Relatives and strangers are always welcome drop-ins at Sugar's. She likes to say, "Any friend of yours is a friend of mine." **Persona:** Sweet-and-Friendly Grandma
Sunny	**(pronounced sun-nee).** She is bright and cheerful. **Persona:** You-Are-My-Sunshine Grandma

Tata	**(pronounced ta-ta).** She is engaging and dismissive at the same time. **Persona:** Gets-Things-Moving Grandma **Fun Fact:** Philanthropist Charlotte Ford, daughter of Henry Ford II, is called Tata.
Techie	**(pronounced tek-ē).** She's usually connected to several devices at once. **Persona:** Techie Grandma
Tita	**(pronounced tē-ta).** She likes to say, "An ounce of mother is worth a pound of clergy." **Persona:** Old-Spanish-Saying Grandma
Tipse	**(pronounced tip-sē).** Occasionally may have one too many. **Persona:** Wine-O'clock Grandma
Tootsie	**(pronounced tŭt-sē).** Tootsie looks forward to her Friday night bar-hopping with coworkers. **Persona:** Never-Grew-Up Grandma

Tricksie	**(pronounced trik-sē).** Tricksie can be somewhat eccentric because she is older and she does not care what people think of her. **Persona:** Drinks-Right-out-of-the-Bottle Grandma
Tutu	**(pronounced tōō-tōō).** She is a humble, plain-spoken woman willing to sacrifice for her grandchildren. Nickname is Toot. **Persona:** Hawaiian Grandma
Tutu Wahine	**(pronounced tōō-tōō-wä-hēn-e).** She is peaceful. **Persona:** Respectful Grandma

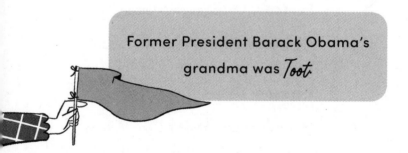

Former President Barack Obama's grandma was *Toot.*

Umma	**(pronounced ōō-mä).** Umma's mixed heritage makes her unique and mysterious. **Persona:** One-Very-Interesting-Background Grandma
Ummy	**(pronounced ōō-mē).** She prefers to stretch her elastic waist pants comfortably over her tummy. **Persona:** Unfashionable Grandma
Uppy	**(pronounced ŭp-pē).** A bit uptight and slightly arrogant. **Persona:** Snooty Grandma

Va	**(pronounced vä).** She likes to say, "Stumbling is not falling." **Persona:** Old-Portuguese-Saying Grandma

Vanna	**(pronounced văn-nă).** A.k.a. the beautiful TV show hostess, Vanna White. Enough said. **Persona:** TV Celebrity Grandma
Vela	**(pronounced vā-lă).** Vela is a dreamer who has big plans for her grandchildren. **Persona:** Wishful-Thinking Latin Grandma **Fun Fact:** Vela is a constellation known as "the Sail."
Vieja	**(pronounced vē-ā-hä).** Literal Spanish translation is "old," but this Vieja brings life to everyone around her! **Persona:** Vivacious Spanish Grandma
Voltage	**(pronounced vol-taj).** Her sharp tongue and quick wit will keep you on your toes. **Persona:** Live-Wire Grandma
Vovo	**(pronounced vō-vō).** A strong woman who is not afraid of hard work or of intimidating people. Her slightly larger hands are indicative of her hardworking Portuguese ancestors. **Persona:** Strong Portuguese Grandma

Walita	**(pronounced wôl-ē-tä).** When highly agitated she reverts back to speaking Spanish (loudly and quickly!). **Persona:** Don't-Get-Me-Started Mexican Grandma
WaiPo	**(pronounced wī-pō).** She listens to spirits. **Persona:** Elder-Ancestor Grandma
WaWa	**(pronounced wä-wä).** Super spunky! **Persona:** Endless-Energy Grandma
Wella	**(pronounced wel-ä).** Wella tries to be "politically correct." She reluctantly traded her mink coat for a faux fur. **Persona:** Trying-to-Be-a-Responsible-Citizen Grandma
Whirly	**(pronounced wurl-ē).** Short for "Whirlwind." **Persona:** Cyclone Grandma

Actress Suzanne Somers was *Zannie.*

Wippe	**(pronounced wip-ē).** Wippe never has a bad word to say about anyone. **Persona:** Sees-Only-the-Good Grandma

Xena	**(pronounced zēn-yə).** Every Halloween, she excitedly puts on her brown leather Xena the Warrior Princess costume. **Persona:** Fantasy Grandma

YaYa	**(pronounced yä-yä).** Her bumper sticker says, "Sexy Greek Senior Citizen." **Persona:** Fun-Loving Greek Grandma
Yella	**(pronounced yel-la).** She's a "yeller." **Persona:** Loud and Opinionated Grandma

YiaYia	**(pronounced yä-yä).** Like the ancient Greek plays of long ago, Yia-Yia can be obscure and controversial. **Persona:** Not-Sure-What-She-Is-Thinking Greek Grandma
Yogie	**(pronounced yōg-ee).** Currently seeking peace and serenity in her grandmother phase of life. **Persona:** Zen Grandma
Yoo-Hoo	**(pronounced yōō-hōō).** She is the dreaded busybody, nosy neighbor who will greet you with a big "Yoo-Hoo!" **Persona:** You-Can-Hear-Her-a-Mile-Away Grandma

Zannie	**(pronounced zān-nē).** Willing to try new, radical youth potions to ward off aging. **Persona:** Celebrity Grandma

ZeeZee	**(pronounced zē-zē).** Has a versatile personality. **Persona:** Movie-Star Grandma **Fun Fact:** Movie star Catherine Zeta-Jones's grandma name is ZeeZee.
Zippy	**(pronounced zip-ē).** Quick and agile. In the backyard, she will still attempt a cartwheel for her grandkids. **Persona:** BENGAY Grandma
Zsa Zsa	**(pronounced zäzä).** She's an exquisite actress and socialite. **Persona:** Hungarian Grandma **Fun Fact:** Zsa Zsa Gabor wedded nine husbands and was the author of *How to Catch a Man, How to Keep a Man,* and *How to Get Rid of a Man.*
ZuZu	**(pronounced zōō-zōō).** She is adorable with her tight, curly, white, cotton ball–shaped hairdo. **Persona:** Just-a-Very-Nice Grandma

Celebrity Grandmas

CELEBRITY GRANDMA	CELEBRITY GRANDMA NAME	CELEBRITY FUN FACT
Kirstie Allie	*Gammy*	An American actress. Her breakout role was as Rebecca Howe in the NBC sitcom *Cheers*, receiving an Emmy Award and a Golden Globe in 1991 for the role.
Jade Jagger	*Jade*	Daughter of Rolling Stones rock star Mick Jagger and former model Bianca Jagger.

NeNe Leakes	*Glamma*	The Real Housewife of Atlanta calls herself a "sassy, fashion-forward Grandma."
Tamra Judge	*Tam-ma*	Tamra is a Real Housewife of Orange County.
Kathie Lee Gifford	*Bubbie*	An American television presenter, singer, songwriter, actress and author. Former *Today Show* host.
Duchess Sarah Ferguson	*Dutchy*	Former wife of Britain's Prince Andrew.
Terry Irwin	*Bunny*	Terry is the widow of the famous "Crocodile Hunter" Steve Irwin.
Fantasia Barrino	*Glam Mom*	Fantasia was the *American Idol* winner in 2004.

Catherine Zeta-Jones	*ZeeZee*	Welsh actress who is known for her versatility; married to American actor, Michael Douglas.
Amy Grant	*Ama*	Amy Grant is an American singer, songwriter, and musician. She has been referred to as "The Queen of Christian Pop."
Christine Brown	*Oma*	Christine is a former *Sister Wives* show star and former wife/sister.
Rosie O'Donnell	*Nana*	An American comedian, television producer, actress, author, and television personality.
Jane Seymour	*Oma*	An English actress. She was a Bond girl in the James Bond film *Live and Let Die* (1973).

Sally Fields	*Grammy*	An American actress who has received two Academy Awards, three Primetime Emmy Awards, two Golden Globe Awards, a Screen Actors Guild Award, a Cannes Film Festival Award for Best Actress, and nominations for a Tony Award and for two British Academy Film Awards.
Judy Blume	*Nonie*	An American writer of children's, young adult, and adult fiction.
Rita Wilson	*YiaYia*	An American actress who is married to American actor Tom Hanks.

Melissa Gilbert	*Nana*	Melissa's (*Little House on the Prairie* actress Laura Ingalls a.k.a. "half-pint") Instagram hashtag is #nanapint.
Gayle King	*Gaia*	American TV personality; best friends with Oprah.
Marie Osmond	*Glamma*	An American singer and actress. She has eight children.

"When nothing is going well,
call your grandmother."

—*Old Italian proverb*

Grandmother Stories

ZENI

One clever grandmother reversed her middle name. Her full name is Sarah Inez Crawford Lee, and her new grandmother name is "Zeni."

LOLLY-POP

One witty grandma decided since grandpa was going to be "Pop," she would be "Lolly," making them "Lolly-Pop."

LULU

Grandma's name was Lucy, but her husband of forty-eight years always called her Lulu and so did her grandchildren. Then, Lulu decided to rename her husband from "Grandpa" to "Papa" because she thought "Lulu & Papa" sounded better together!

SASSY

One grandma, who owns a house on the Connecticut shore, loves sailing with her grandkids and world traveling. She declared that her rightful, perfectly apt grandma name would be "Sassy." So, Sassy it is.

Amazing Grandmas

OLDEST MOM

The world's oldest mom is Omkari Panwar. She was seventy-two when she gave birth to twins in India in 2008. The world's second oldest mom is Rosanna Dalla Corte. She was sixty-three when she gave birth in Italy in 1994.

ATHLETIC GRANDMA

Sue Oldham, a sixty-four-year-old Perth grandmother, became the oldest woman to swim the English Channel on August 9, 2010. She completed the crossing in 17 hours and 31 minutes.

QUEEN OF ROCK 'N ROLL GRANDMA

Tina Turner, a grandma and great-grandma, rocked skin-tight outfits and spiked heels at her sold-out concerts!

INTERNET GRANDMA

Maria Amelia Lopez, a grandmother from Spain, became an Internet sensation after dubbing herself the "world's oldest blogger." At the

time of her death on 20 May 2009 aged ninety-seven, she had a blog attracting 1.7 million visitors.

Famous Grandmas

RUTH BADER GINSBERG – *Bubbie*

One of America's most prolific women, RBG (as she was lovingly called), was an esteemed Supreme Court Justice since the age of sixty. She was the leading voice for gender equality, women's interests, and civil rights and liberties. She embodied the strength, intelligence, character, and steadfastness of arguably the most notable supreme court justice of the 21st century. Her grandchildren called her "Bubbie."

GRANDMA MOSES – *Famous Artist Grandma*

This famous folk artist was widely known for her "primitive American" style. She had thirty grandchildren, and along with her considerable progeny, she left the world a considerable body of work. Though she didn't begin to paint until age seventy-six, she produced more than 3,600 canvases.

MARIAN ROBINSON – *"First" Granny*

Some media outlets have dubbed her "first granny." Former First Lady Michelle Obama's mom, Marian Robinson, was the unquestioned live-in taskmaster of her two granddaughters while in the White House. "I am standing here breathing in and out with any level of calm because my 70-year-old [mother] is home with my girls," Michelle said on the campaign trail (February 2008). "There's nothing like grandma."

MONA IN "WHO'S THE BOSS?'" – *Mona*

Katherine Helmond may have played Alyssa Milano's grandma in the long-running Tony Danza sitcom *Who's the Boss?*, but her character simply went by "Mona"—not "Grandma." Helmond also had a recurring role as Ray Romano's mother-in-law in *Everybody Loves Raymond*. But the actress, also known for the TV series *Soap* (1977–1981) and for Terry Gilliam movies such as *Time Bandits* and *Brazil*, Had to really act in those roles: she had no children in real life.

RHODELL TERRY – *Marathon Grandma*

At seventy-five years old, Rhodell Terry decided she needed to celebrate by running a marathon in Pine Valley, Utah. She was also a mother of ten, grandmother of thirty-eight, and a great-grandmother. At age seventy, she become a volunteer firefighter and achieved an advanced EMT certificate to support her beloved community.

CHAU SMITH – *Ultra Marathon Grandma*

With her seventieth birthday fast approaching, Chau Smith signed up for a truly amazing race: seven marathons in seven consecutive days on seven continents, also known as the Triple 7 Quest. Chau Smith is a five-foot-tall Kansas City grandmother and a Vietnamese immigrant who survived war, divorce, poverty, and years as a single mother in a foreign country, and this was just another challenge she would overcome one step at a time. "I didn't want to make a political statement," Smith said, "But as a mother, as a grandmother…I wanted to run to represent women."

LARRY JOHNSON – *Grandmama*

This NBA star donned grandma's gear (floral dress, pearls, cat-eyeglasses, and a pillbox hat) for a famous 1993 Converse commercial. When not playing "Grandmama," Johnson was the defensive rebound leader for the Charlotte Hornets and appeared in the movies *Space Jam* and *Eddie*.

DEIRDRE LARKIN – *Running Grandma*

At seventy-eight, Deirdre was diagnosed with advanced osteoporosis and prescribed medication. The medication made her so ill that Deirdre decided to take up running to prevent bone loss. Once her feet hit the ground, there was no stopping her. She broke the 10 km record for South African women over seventy, as well as the world record for women over eighty with a time of 54 minutes and 17 seconds. She turned ninety on September 24, 2021, and is still running strong.

GRIETJE SCOTT –

Brave and Decorated Grandma

Grietje Scott was a highly decorated member of the Dutch underground and part of an elite fighting force during WWII. She and her family hid Jewish neighbors for protection during the war. She never told anyone (about her past) until she was ninety years old. Her Grandma name was "Kieks."

International Grandmother Names

Family history, culture, and traditions are important legacies that grandparents pass down from generation to generation. Choosing a name that represents your family history is one way to carry on a piece of your heritage!

AFRICAN

Ouma (Kenya)

Makhulu (Venda)

Ugogo (Zula)

Gogo (Zula)

Nyanya (Swahili)

Nkuku (Botswana)

AMERICAN INDIAN

Amá Sání (Navajo)

BOSNIAN

Baba

Baka

Nena

CHINESE

Nai Nai

(father's mother)

PoPo

Wai Po

(maternal grandma)

Lao Lao

(mother's mother)

Aana

Bubu

Babicka

Yalewa

Babi

Lola

Bestemor

Nanay

Fafa

Mormor

Isoäiti

Mummi

Grootmoeder

Mummo

Teta

Bomma

Bommi

Aanak

(Inuit—paternal

grandma)

Grand Maman

Ananaksaq

Grand-mère

(maternal grandma)

Mémère

Aanaga

Mamie

Mémé

GERMAN

Grossmutter

Oma

Omi

Beste Moder

Groosma

Groosmutter

GREEK

Gigia

Yaya

YiaYia

HAWAIIAN

Toot

Tutu

Tutu Wahine

HEBREW

Savta

Safta

HINDI

Daadi ma

Nani

ICELANDIC

Amma

INDIAN

Ajji

Dadi

Dida

INDONESIAN

Nenek

IRISH

Grand Mum

Maimeó

Máthair Mhór

Máthair Chríona

Móraí

Seanmháthair

ITALIAN

Nonna

Nonnie

Nonnina

JAPANESE

Baachan

Obachan

Sobo

Obaba

KOREAN

Halmoni

NORWEGIAN

Bestemor

Gammlemor

Oldemore

Farmor

Mormor

POLISH

Babci

Babcia

Busia

Babula

PORTUGUESE

Avó

Vovo

Vo

ROMANIAN

Bunica

Mamaia (Granny)

RUSSIAN

Babushka

SCOTTISH

Mhamo

Seanmhair

SERBIAN

Baba

Baca (Granny)

Mica

SPAIN

Avia

Laia

SPANISH

Abuela

Abuelita

Lala Manita

Lita

SWEDISH

Farmor

Mormor

Phar-Mor

TAIWANESE

Ama

Neima

Waima

TURKISH

Anneanne

Baabanne

Buyukanne

UKRAINIAN

Baba

Babusia

VIETNAMESE

Ba

Ba Ngoai

YIDDISH

Bubbe

Bubbie

Grandmother Names by Personality

CEREBRAL

Beeta

Mae

Mica

Mummy

Tita

Wella

CRAFTY

Bree

Golly

Gumma

Mummi

Ninna

Xena

ENERGETIC

Bibi

Birdie

Coco

Dodo

Galini

Lola

CLASSY

Didi

Gigi

Lady

Mémère

Mimi

Vela

DOMESTIC

Bana

Gada

Grossmutter

Ma

Marme

Tutu

FUN

Beemie

Chickie

Gabby

Glamma

Goose

Jiggy

SPORTY

Cici

Gogo

Juju

Lilly

Moxiemom

Plucky

ROMANTIC

Bella

Bubbles

Gaia

Goddess

Ona Great

Wella

MODERN

Big Mama

Egge

Frannie

Gammommie

MeMom

Tootsie

TRADITIONAL

Babka

Grammy

Grandma

Nana

Nonna

Oma

STUFFY

Binky

Bitsy

Contessa

Duchess

Fifi

Grand Meir

SOCIAL

Dolly

Evie

Fancy

Ginny

Sugar

Sunny

Perfect Pairs:

GRANDMA AND GRANDPA NAMES
THAT GO TOGETHER PERFECTLY

Airy—Ace

Bebe—Bear

Birdie—Bogey

Bitsy—Itsy

Bossie—Boss

Bubbe—Zayde

Chickie—Coach

Chickie—Farfar

Cici—Captain

Coco—Puff

Dame—Duke

Didi—Baba

Ditti—Doc

Duchess—Duke

Gigi—Gramps

Gigi—Poppi

Glamma—Glampa

Granny—Grampy

Gram—Crackers

Happy—Grumpy

Huggie—Bear

Indy—Chief

Jumpy—Lumpy

Juno—Jupiter

Lolly—Pop

Lucy—Ricky

MeMaw—MePaw

Mimi—Ace

Mimi—Mate

MopMop—PopPop

Nana—Papa

Nanoo—Papoo

Queenie—Ace

Queenie—King

Sassy—Pappy

Sugar—Big Daddy

Tickles—Pickles

YaYa—PaPa

"Enjoy the little things, for one day
you may look back and realize they were
the big things."

—*Robert Brault, author*

GRANDMA'S GRANDBABY PLANNER

When it comes to something as important as a new grandbaby, it is always a good idea to be as organized as possible before arrival. The checklist below is a super helpful tool to ensure you are ready for the big day and the days following shortly after!

1-3 months prior to baby's due date

☐ Find out the date of the "baby" shower and mark your calendar.

- Review their baby registry and purchase item(s).
- Find your son's or daughter's favorite old baby blanket, rattle, stuffed animal, etc., to share and/ or gift to the parent as a wonderful memento of when they were a baby.

- [ ] Inquire if a baby "reveal" party is also planned. If yes, find out the date.
- [ ] Identify a girlfriend who will gladly host your "Grandma-to-Be" shower!
  - Make sure your grandma-to-be shower date is AFTER the "baby" shower and "reveal" party.
  - Grandma's REGISTRY (list of necessary baby items for Grandma's house).

EQUIPMENT

- Portable crib (Pack 'n Play)
- Car seat (convertible from infant to toddler)
- Exersaucer
- High chair
- Bouncy seat
- Stroller
- Baby gate

ACCESSORIES

- Bibs
- Burp cloths
- Baby blankets
- Diapers
- Diaper wipes warmer
- Changing pad
- Thermometer
- Breakproof bowls & spoons
- White noise machine
- Books, toys, stuffed animals

- ☐ Let your "Grandma-to-Be" shower host know where you have registered.
- ☐ After your "Grandma-to-Be" shower, send handwritten thank-you notes.
- ☐ Wash and clean all new baby equipment and accessories.

One week prior to due date

- ☐ Make sure you understand the birth plan and ask nicely how you can help.
- ☐ Find old baby photos or the baby book of your son or daughter when they were born.
- ☐ Make sure you fully understand how to take photos with your phone or iPad; practice.
- ☐ Update phone contact list—family, friends, neighbors.
- ☐ Create text groups for easy texting about baby's arrival!
- ☐ Buy an extra phone charger to always carry with you and your phone.
- ☐ Make sure you fully understand how to text and email new baby photos to family & friends.
- ☐ Install infant car seat—be ready!
  - Go to local fire station for infant car seat inspection (make sure it is installed correctly!).

A few days before

- ☐ Grocery shop to cook and freeze a few favorite meals for new parents.

- ☐ Find out name & tele number of a few local restaurants (near the new parents) that deliver.

  - Italian: _____

  - Mexican: _____

  - Greek: _____

  - Japanese: _____

  - Chinese: _____

  - Deli (sandwiches): _____

  - Pizza: _____

  - Bagels/Bakery: _____

- ☐ Have phone charged and with you at all times.

- ☐ Gas up car.

- ☐ Keep CALM!

Day of baby's arrival

- ☐ Have phone charged and with you at ALL times! THIS IS YOUR ONE JOB TODAY!

Days following baby's arrival

- ☐ Have phone with you at all times to answer panicked questions from new parents.
- ☐ Be on-call for emergency questions and concerns from the new parents.
- ☐ Bring your son or daughter's baby book over to the new parents so they can see how they grew.
- ☐ Drop off prepared meals.
- ☐ Schedule food deliveries—groceries and/or meals.
- ☐ Bring over coffee/tea, fruit, bagels or doughnuts for an AM pick-me-up for Mom and Dad.
- ☐ Be readily available at a moment's notice.

Grandma's Playbook

E very winning team has an amazing coach or strong leader who understands their players' characteristics—their personality, beliefs, motivation, interests, and perceptions—and carefully works strategically on their playbook to ensure a successful team.

As a new grandma or grandma-to-be, your success will be determined by carefully examining your family characteristics, specifically your daughter or daughters-in-law, and creating your new "Grandma Playbook and Planner."

The following guide will assist you with understanding the parents-to-be characteristics and provide suggested advice for creating your own customized playbook. Your playbook is your own guide to becoming a well-loved and respected grandma!

Parents-to-Be Category & Characteristics	Grandma's Playbook
Gen Z • Technically savvy • "Me" generation • Likes to travel • Life experiences are important • Gets parenting advice ONLINE	Get an iPad ASAP and practice Facetiming with your girlfriends! Speak your mind! They will either listen or completely disregard; they will take no offense. Texting is the best way to communicate with them. Be supportive; offer babysitting.
Millennial • Competitive • Nostalgic • Husband/Dad-to-be helps out	Know the latest & greatest baby products—be hip! Reminisce about the '80s and '90s. Ask the DAD if he needs help or relief—score big here! Be available.

Helicopter	Speak only when spoken to—offer no unsolicited advice!
• Pays extreme attention to educational development	
• Overschedules	Have unscripted, fun-spirited outings with grandchild.
• Dislikes unpleasant or challenging situations for child	When alone with grandchild, encourage independent thinking.
	No Disney-animated movies or books.
	Educational book reading only.
Tiger	Be kind and gentle when approaching.
• Can be overly protective	
• Can be authoritative	Always bring food when visiting.
	Ensure parent of your safe environment for grandkids.
	Respect rules, but quietly tell stories to grandkids of "how it used to be back in the day."

Snowplow	Stay out of their way!
• Removes all roadblocks for child	Leave the parenting to the parents.
• May have delusional Princess or Prince thoughts about child	Schedule one-on-one time for normal, fun-time activities with grandma.

Be understanding. |

Dos, Don'ts, and Advice

Review the following tips to ensure effective communication with the new parents—let's make sure your Grandmotherhood journey gets off to a GREAT start!

DO THIS:

- Offer (don't insist) to babysit.
- Help around the house—fold laundry, load the dishwasher, take out the trash & recycling.
- Walk and feed the dog.
- Pay attention to the other grandchildren.
- Voice no opinions. If you aren't asked for one, don't offer one up. Ever.
- Run a few errands—grocery store, pharmacy, farmers market.
- Take pictures, but don't post pictures without permission.
- Ogle over the baby.

- Be supportive from a distance.
- Know your boundaries.
- Tell the new mom she's doing a great job.

DON'T DO THIS:

- Don't clean up her house without asking first.
- Don't give unsolicited advice.
- If you are given a key to their home, use it sparingly.
- Don't drop in without calling or texting.
- Don't assume that you'll be invited along on trips and vacations.
- Don't expect to be invited to every party and social occasion.
- Don't ask about the "next one."
- Don't overwhelm with excessive amounts of gifts.
- Don't withhold your love.

ADVICE:

Grandmothers are still the reliable, go-to source for tried-and-true advice! Here are a few truisms that grandmothers still swear by today:

- If you don't have anything nice to say, don't say it at all.
- Mind your manners.

- You're beautiful, inside and out.

- Do what makes you happy.

- Everything in moderation.

- Be nice to your siblings; in the end that's all you'll have

- This too shall pass.

- Shoulders back, chin up.

- Believe in yourself and think positively.

- Sometimes less is more.

- Everything happens for a reason.

- Take care of your skin.

- Say please and thank you.

- You catch more flies with honey than vinegar.

- Don't say "goodbye." just "see you later."

Final Fun Fact: The World Needs Grandmothers to Survive

Grandmothers throughout history have known what is now formally called the "Grandmother Hypothesis." It is a theory that grandmothers helped young children (grandchildren) to develop better social skills, create special bonding relationships and learn new skills that led to bigger brains and longer lifespans.

How were they able to do it? *MENOPAUSE.*

What?! Yes. The theory explains that without menopause, older women would simply continue to have children, instead of acting as grandmothers. Grandmothers (historically) helped collect food, feed, and take care of the very young grandchildren, enabling mothers to have more children. As a result, grandmothers became very necessary and important supplementary caregivers as well as furthering human population and evolution.

In a nutshell, grandmothers increased and continue to increase everyone's survival rate!

Just another reason to be thankful for Grandmothers!

Grandma Notes

Acknowledgments

F irst, to my mother "Bubbe," for her unwavering and steadfast determination to claim her rightful grandmother name.

To my children, Kelly Ann and Will, who lived through mounds of papers everywhere and hours of seemingly endless writing and editing. Without their love, support, and understanding, I would have never completed this book.

To my fun, adventurous friend Cathy Swett, who designed the fabulous grandma drawings for my first, self-published book edition.

To my neighbor and literary expert, Nancy Perlman, who unselfishly gave of her time to guide me through this complicated literary process.

To every friend and friend-of-friend who took the time to tell me their wonderful grandmother names and stories. It is because of your generosity this book is true and authentic.

Lastly, to everyone who ever asked me, "How's your book

coming along?" It truly inspired and encouraged me to keep going and greatly motivated me to finish this project. For that and more, I am so grateful.

Index

About the Author

Cathy Livingstone believes that today's grandmothers are women-on-the-go, working hard, playing hard, and looking good. She grew up west of Boston (Belmont, MA) and received her computer science degree from The College of William and Mary (Williamsburg, VA). Her work has been featured in the *Washington Post*, *Grand Magazine*, and *Oklahoma Lifestyles 50+*. She currently resides in Montclair, New Jersey.